Spanish Basics, Book 1

NOMBRE (Name):

_____

ESCUELA (School):

_____

Table of Contents

Mi Camino Spanish™
El Camino Spanish LLC
info@micaminospanish.com

Teacher Tip! For multimedia resources to support delivery of these lessons including lesson slides, learning games, links to YouTube videos, lesson plans and more, please send an email to info@micaminospanish.com or check out my store at www.teacherspayteachers.com!

 ISBN 978-1-365-87855-8

Lesson 1 – Greetings, Good-byes & Introduction to "SER"

What will we learn in this lesson?

By the end of this lesson, you will be able to:

- Use Spanish personal pronouns
- Explain the difference between "tú" and "usted"
- Use common Spanish greetings
- Use common Spanish good-byes
- Use common Spanish phrases to introduce yourself
- Conjugate the verb "SER" (to be) in the present tense
- Explain how "HAY" (there is/there are) is used

Los Pronombres Personales (Personal Pronouns)

I	Yo
You	Tú
He / She / You (formal)	Él / Ella / Usted (Ud.)
We	Nosotros/as
You all (informal)	Vosotros/as
They / They (girls) / You all (formal)	Ellos / Ellas / Ustedes (Uds.)

> Hey y'all! "Vosotros" is used only in Spain!

Tú vs. Usted

In Spanish, there are two ways to say "you." One is informal, or the "you" that you would use with friends and close family, and the other is formal, or the "you" that you would use with teachers, grown-ups, or people you would normally treat more respectfully.

"Tú"

INFORMAL – With friends and close family, use "tú."

FORMAL – With grown-ups, teachers, and anyone deserving more respect, use "usted."

"Usted"

Common Greetings

Mister or Sir	Señor
Mrs. or Ma'am	Señora
Miss	Señorita
Good day. / Good morning.	Buenos días.
Good evening. / Good night.	Buenas noches.
Good afternoon.	Buenas tardes.
Hello.	Hola.
Welcome.	Bienvenido/os/a/as

"Hola. Me llamo Miguel."

"Hola. Me llamo Jose. Mucho gusto."

How are you?	¿Cómo está (usted)? (formal)
	¿Cómo estás (tú)? (informal)
How are ya? (casual)	¿Qué tal?
How's it going?	¿Cómo te va? (informal)
Well. / Very well.	Bien. / Muy bien.
So so.	Así así.
More or less.	Más o menos.
Bad. / Very bad.	Mal. / Muy mal.
And you?	¿Y usted? (formal)
	¿Y tú? (informal)

Common Good-byes

Goodbye.	Adiós.
Until later.	Hasta luego.
Until tomorrow.	Hasta mañana.
Until soon.	Hasta pronto.
We'll see you.	Nos vemos.

"Adiós."

Introductions & Self-Identification

What is your name?	¿Cómo se llama usted? (formal)
	¿Cómo te llamas tú? (informal)
My name is…	Me llamo…
	Mi nombre es…
I am…	Yo soy…
Where are you from?	¿De dónde es usted? (formal)
	¿De dónde eres tú? (informal)
I'm from…	Soy de…
I'm from the U.S.	Soy de los Estados Unidos.
Nice to meet you.	Mucho gusto.
The pleasure is mine.	El gusto es mío.
It's been a pleasure.	Ha sido un placer.
Same to you.	Igualmente.

Being Polite

Please.	Por favor.
Thank you.	Gracias.
Thank you very much.	Muchas gracias.
Than you very, very much!	Muchísimas gracias.
You're welcome.	De nada.

"Muchas gracias."

"De nada."

ROLE PLAY

Scenario #1:

You run into a friend at school.

Say in Spanish:

YOU: "Hola. ¿Qué tal?"

YOUR FRIEND: "Bien, ¿Cómo estás?"

YOU: "Bien gracias."

Scenario #2:

You walk into your class in the morning and greet your teacher.

Say in Spanish:

YOU: "Buenos días. ¿Cómo está usted?"

YOUR TEACHER: "Muy bien, ¿y tú?"

YOU: "Estoy bien. Gracias."

Scenario #3:

You see another kid in your neighborhood.

Say in Spanish:

YOU: "Hola. ¿Qué tal?"

KID: "Hola. ¿Cómo te llamas?"

YOU: "Me llamo Miguel. ¿Cómo te llamas tú?"

KID: "Me llamo Jose."

YOU: "Mucho gusto."

KID: "Mucho gusto."

Scenario #4:

Talking to other students in your class, or your teacher, practice using greetings & good-byes.

Introduction to "SER" (To Be)

The verb "SER" means "TO BE" in Spanish. We use SER to describe or to introduce others and ourselves. Let's learn how to conjugate this important verb in the present tense!

I am	Yo **SOY**
You are	Tú **ERES**
He / She / You (formal) are	Él / Ella / Usted (Ud.) **ES**
We are	Nosotros/as **SOMOS**
You all (informal) are	Vosotros/as **SOIS**
They / You all (formal) are	Ellos / Ellas / Ustedes (Uds.) **SON**

IMPORTANT NOTE: We will discuss verb conjugation and talk more about the verb "SER" in future lessons. For now, just understand that verb conjugation is an essential Spanish grammar skill that takes lots of practice!

Introduction to "HAY" (There is/There are)

The use of "hay" in Spanish simply means, "there is" or "there are." It is pronounced exactly like "eye" in English. Whether there is one or many, "hay" stays the same:

> "There is one dog." – "Hay un perro."

> "There are many dogs." – "Hay muchos perros."

Use "hay" every time you would use "there is" or "there are" when translating from English.

"Hay un perro."

"Hay muchos perros."

Lesson Summary

I know how to use Spanish personal pronouns!

> **Yo** (I), **Tú** (you informal), **Él** (he), **Ella** (she), **Usted** (you formal), **Nosotros/as** (we), **Vosotros/as** (you all used only in Spain), **Ellos/Ellas** (they), & **Ustedes** (you all).

I can explain the difference between "tú" and "usted!"

> There are two ways to say "you" in Spanish; one is formal and one is informal. With friends & family I use **"tú"** and with grown-ups, teachers, & anyone deserving more respect, I use **"usted."**

I can use common Spanish greetings!

> There are many ways to greet people in Spanish, just like in English. Some common greetings are: **"buenos días"** (good day/good morning), **"buenas tardes"** (good afternoon), and **"buenas noches"** (good evening or good night).

I can use common Spanish good-byes!

> Some ways that I can say "good-bye" in Spanish are: **"adiós"** (good-bye), **"hasta luego"** (until later), and **"nos vemos"** (we'll see you).

I can use common Spanish phrases to introduce myself!

> There are many phrases I can use to introduce myself like, **"Me llamo…"** (My name is…), **"Soy de los Estados Unidos"** (I am from the United States), and **"Mucho gusto"** (nice to meet you).

I can conjugate the verb "SER" (to be) in the present tense!

> **Yo SOY** (I am), **Tú ERES** (you are), **Él/Ella/Usted ES** (he/she is, you are), **Nosotros/as SOMOS** (we are), **Vosotros/as SOIS** (you all are), **Ellos/Ellas/Ustedes SON** (they/you all are).

I can explain how "HAY" (there is / there are) is used!

> "Hay" is used when saying "there is" or "there are." It doesn't change from singular to plural.

SPANISH GREETINGS & GOOD-BYES CROSSWORD PUZZLE

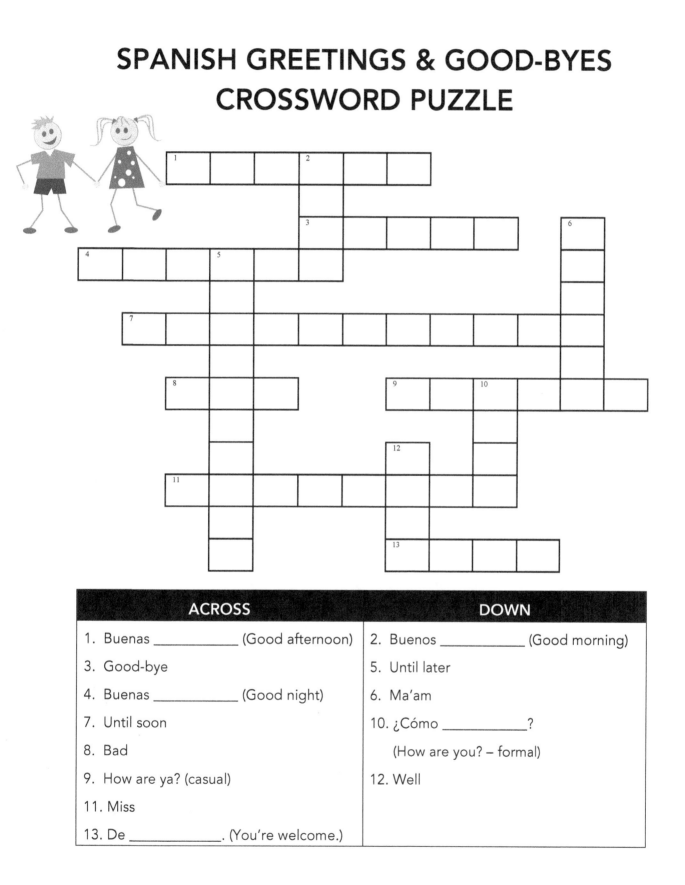

ACROSS	DOWN
1. Buenas _____ (Good afternoon)	2. Buenos _____ (Good morning)
3. Good-bye	5. Until later
4. Buenas _____ (Good night)	6. Ma'am
7. Until soon	10. ¿Cómo _____?
8. Bad	(How are you? – formal)
9. How are ya? (casual)	12. Well
11. Miss	
13. De _____. (You're welcome.)	

SPANISH PERSONAL PRONOUNS & SER WORKSHEET

Fill in the chart below with the Spanish personal pronouns. Use the word bank to help!

Él   **Ellos**   **Nosotros**

Usted   **Ustedes**   **Ellas**

Tú   **Vosotros**

Ella   **Yo**

I		WE	
YOU (familiar)		YOU ALL (familiar)	
HE		THEY (boys)	
SHE		THEY (girls)	
YOU (formal)		YOU ALL (formal)	

Fill in the chart below with the proper form of the verb "SER". Use the word bank to help! NOTE: In some cases, you will use the conjugated verb more than once.

Soy   **Son**   **Es**

Eres   **Somos**   **Sois**

Yo		Nosotros	
Tú		Vosotros	
Él		Ellos	
Ella		Ellas	
Usted		Ustedes	

GREETINGS & GOOD-BYE'S
VOCABULARY REVIEW

1. Draw a line to the correct Spanish word or phrase!

Goodbye.   Hasta luego.

Until later.   Nos vemos.

Until tomorrow.   Hasta pronto.

Until soon.   Adiós.

We'll see you.   Hasta mañana.

2. Tú vs. Usted - ¿Cierto o Falso? (True or False)

Write "CIERTO" or "FALSO" next to the following statements:

I would use "tú" with my best friend.   _____

I would use "usted" with my sister.   _____

I would use "usted" with my teacher.   _____

I would use "tú" with the principal.   _____

I would use "usted" with my little cousin.   _____

3. Circle the appropriate response to the following questions:

"¿Qué tal? (circle one)

- Me llamo Juan.   • Nos vemos.

- Bien, ¿y tú?   • Buenas noches.

¿De dónde eres? (circle one)

- Ha sido un placer.   • Mucho gusto.

- Soy de Costa Rica.   • Igualmente.

4. What does "hay" mean in Spanish?

- There is.

- There are.

- Both

5. In what country is "vosotros" used?

- Mexico
- Spain
- Costa Rica
- France

6. Circle the phrases that are considered common Spanish greetings.

- Buenos días.
- Buenas tardes.
- Hasta luego.
- Hola, "¿Cómo te va?

7. Find the following words or phrases in this word search.

HOLA   BUENOS DIAS   ADIOS
COMO ESTA   HASTA LUEGO   BUENAS NOCHES
QUE TAL   NOS VEMOS
GRACIAS   BIEN

B	U	I	S	D	I	T	R	H	O	L	A	S	H	S
B	J	S	T	Q	U	E	T	A	L	M	O	D	A	B
R	S	G	R	A	C	I	A	S	R	T	U	N	M	E
A	R	T	U	I	F	H	G	T	U	T	R	O	S	A
B	U	E	N	O	S	D	I	A	S	L	A	S	H	O
C	O	M	O	E	S	T	A	L	M	U	C	V	H	G
M	A	R	A	D	O	O	P	U	S	B	I	E	N	O
G	R	D	R	A	I	O	P	E	H	O	P	M	S	A
N	O	V	O	R	D	U	M	G	S	T	A	O	A	S
G	B	U	E	N	A	S	N	O	C	H	E	S	T	A

Lesson 2 – Numbers, Alphabet, Colors & Shapes

What will we learn in this lesson?

By the end of this lesson, you will be able to:

- Count from 1-20
- Count from 20-30
- Count by 10's to 100
- Count by 100's to 1000
- Say the Spanish Alphabet
- Answer the question, ¿Cuántos hay?
- Say several colors in Spanish!
- Say several shapes in Spanish!

Los Números (1-20)

1	Uno	11	Once
2	Dos	12	Doce
3	Tres	13	Trece
4	Cuatro	14	Catorce
5	Cinco	15	Quince
6	Seis	16	Dieciséis
7	Siete	17	Diecisiete
8	Ocho	18	Dieciocho
9	Nueve	19	Diecinueve
10	Diez	20	Veinte

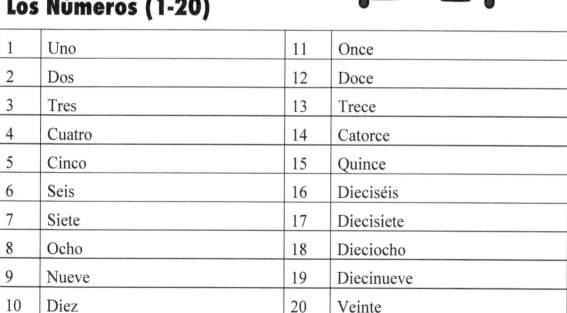

¿Cuántos años tienes? (How old are you?) EXAMPLE: "Yo tengo diez años." (I am 10 years old.)

Los Números (21-39)

21	Veintiuno	31	Treinta-y-uno
22	Veintidos	32	Treinta-y-dos
23	Veintitres	33	Treinta-y-tres
24	Veinticuatro	34	Treinta-y-cuatro
25	Veinticinco	35	Treinta-y-cinco
26	Veintiseis	36	Treinta-y-seis
27	Veintisiete	37	Treinta-y-siete
28	Veintiocho	38	Treinta-y-ocho
29	Veintinueve	39	Treinta-y-nueve
30	Treinta		*Pattern repeats up to 100.*

Los Números (10-1000)

10	Diez	200	Doscientos
20	Veinte	300	Trescientos
30	Treinta	400	Cuatrocientos
40	Cuarenta	500	Quinientos
50	Cincuenta	600	Seiscientos
60	Sesenta	700	Setecientos
70	Setenta	800	Ochocientos
80	Ochenta	900	Novecientos
90	Noventa	1000	Mil
100	Cien		

Write out the following numbers in Spanish:

35 _____

24 _____

46 _____

73 _____

82 _____

El Alfabeto (Alphabet)

a	b	c	ch	d	e	f	g	h	i
j	k	l	ll	m	n	ñ	o	p	q
r	rr	s	t	u	v	w	x	y	z

Las Vocales (Vowels)

a	e	i	o	u

PRACTICE "¿Cómo se deletrea tu nombre?"

How do you spell your name? Working with a friend, practice spelling your name out loud in Spanish. Then, have your friend do the same. For an added challenge, spell your last name too!

¡Los Colores! (Colors)

Red   Rojo

Orange   Naranjo/a

Yellow   Amarillo

Purple   Morado

White   Blanco/a

Black   Negro/a

Blue   Azul

Green   Verde

Pink   Rosa

Brown   Marrón

¿Cuál es tu color favorito? (What is your favorite color?)

EXAMPLE: "Mi color favorito es azul." (My favorite color is blue.)

Using Colors in Spanish

In Spanish, when we use colors to describe something, we need to remember to make sure the color "agrees" with the noun, meaning whether or not the noun is feminine or masculine, singular or plural.

For example, let's take a look at how we describe the color of a feminine noun vs. a masculine noun, and a singular noun vs. a plural noun. How does that affect how we describe its color?

1) **LA MANZANA** (feminine, singular) vs. **LAS MANZANAS** (feminine, plural)

"La manzana es **roja**." – Meaning, "The apple is red."

"Las manzanas son **rojas**." – Meaning, "The apples are red."

2) **EL LIBRO** (masculine, singular) vs. **LOS LIBROS** (masculine, plural)

"El libro es **rojo**." – Meaning, "The book is red."

"Los libros son **rojos**." – Meaning, "The books are red."

Las Formas (Shapes)

Let's learn the names of some basic shapes in Spanish!

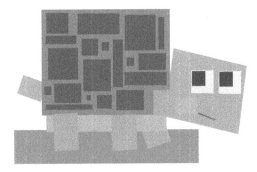

Square	El cuadrado
Circle	El círculo
Triangle	El triángulo
Rectangle	El rectángulo
Heart	El corazón
Star	La estrella
Diamond	El diamante

Lesson Summary

I can count from 1-20 in Spanish!

I can count from 20-30 in Spanish!

I can count by 10's from 10-100 in Spanish!

I can count by 100's from 100-1000 in Spanish!

I can say the Spanish alphabet!

I can say several colors in Spanish!

I can say several shapes in Spanish!

¿Cuántos hay?

Look at each of the pictures and answer the question, ¿Cuántos hay? (How many are there?) Follow the example.

¿Cuántos pájaros hay? *Hay dos pájaros.*

¿Cuántos peces hay? _____

¿Cuántas ranas hay? _____

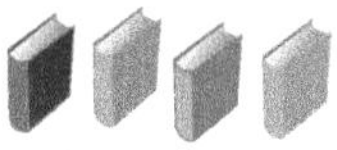

¿Cuántos libros hay? _____

¿Cuántos globos hay? _____

¿Cuántas flores hay? _____

¿Cuántos diamantes hay? _____

¿Cuántos pollitos hay? _____

¿Cuántas velas hay? _____

¿Cuántas mariposas hay? _____

SPANISH COLORS WORKSHEET

Color each splat of paint with one of the colors listed below. Then write in the names of the colors in Spanish below each splat. Use the word bank!

Rojo   Blanco   Rosa
Naranjo   Negro   Marrón
Amarillo   Azul
Morado   Verde

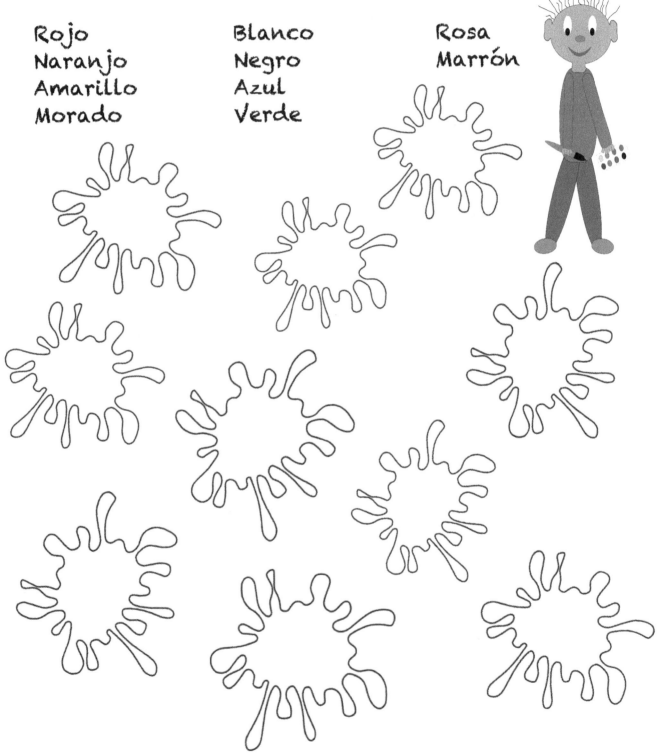

SPANISH COLORS WORKSHEET

Finish the following sentences using the proper form of the color in Spanish taking into account whether or not the noun is masculine or feminine, singular or plural!

1. El plátano es

_____
(yellow)

2. La flor es

_____
(red)

3. Las ranas son

_____
(green)

4. Las uvas son

_____
(purple)

5. Las nubes son

_____
(white)

6. El auto es

_____
(red)

7. El perro es

_____
(brown)

8. Las flores son

_____
(pink)

9. El zapato es

_____
(black)

10. La camisa es

_____
(orange)

SPANISH SHAPES WORKSHEET

Color in the shapes based on the following sentences:

1. El círculo es amarillo.
2. La estrella es azul.
3. El corazón es rojo.
4. El cuadrado es negro.
5. El rectángulo es verde.
6. El triángulo es morado.
7. El diamante es anaranjado.

Then, label each shape in Spanish!

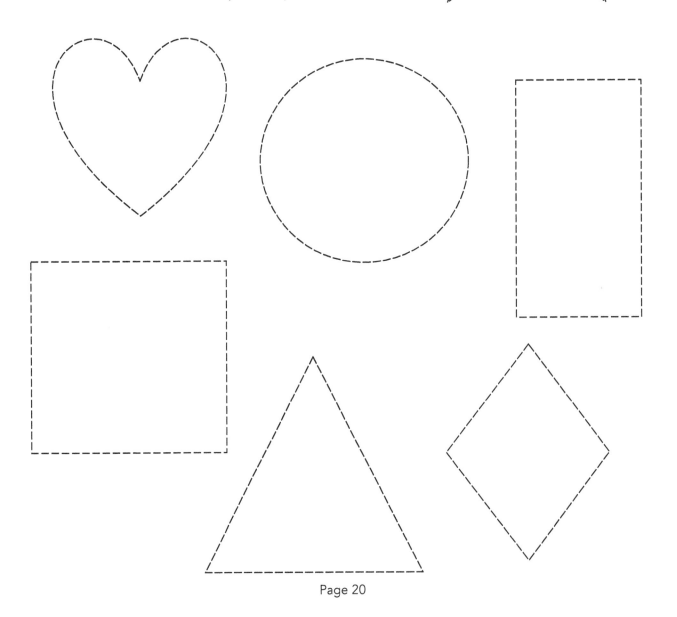

Lesson 3 – The Calendar & Weather Basics

What will we learn in this lesson?

By the end of this lesson, you will be able to:
- Say the days of the week,
- Say the months of the year,
- Say the seasons, and
- Describe the weather in Spanish!
- Answer the question, "¿Qué día es hoy?"
- Answer the question, "¿Qué tiempo hace?"

El Calendario (The Calendar)

Let's look at some essential Spanish vocabulary related to the calendar: days of the week, months of the year, and seasons! Practice saying each vocabulary word out loud in Spanish.

Los Días de la Semana (Days of the Week)

Monday	lunes
Tuesday	martes
Wednesday	miércoles
Thursday	jueves
Friday	viernes
Saturday	sábado
Sunday	domingo

Los Meses del Año (Months of the Year)

January	enero	July	julio
February	febrero	August	agosto
March	marzo	September	septiembre
April	abril	October	octubre
May	mayo	November	noviembre
June	junio	December	diciembre

Las Estaciones (The Seasons)

Winter	El invierno
Spring	La primavera
Summer	El verano
Fall	El otoño

> **IMPORTANT NOTE:** Unlike in English, we do not capitalize days, months, or seasons in Spanish!

Calendar Vocabulary

Day	El día
Week	La semana
Month	El mes
Year	El año
Yesterday	Ayer
Today	Hoy
Tomorrow	Mañana
Season	La estación
Date	La fecha
2017	Dos mil diecisiete
What is the date?	¿Qué es la fecha?
What is today?	¿Qué día es hoy?
Today is the (number) of (month). / Today is the 25th of January.	Hoy es el (número) de (mes). / Hoy es el veinticinco de enero.

¿Qué día es hoy? _____

¿Qué día es mañana? _____

¿Qué es la fecha hoy? _____

¿Cuál es la estación? _____

El Tiempo (The Weather)

When describing the weather in Spanish, we use the verb "hacer" meaning to make or to do. For example, if we want to say it's hot in Spanish, we say "Hace calor." If we want to say it's cold, we say "Hace frío." Think of it as the weather "makes" a certain condition. ¿Qué tiempo hace hoy? Meaning, "What's the weather like today?

Weather Vocabulary

Weather	El tiempo
What's the weather like?	¿Qué tiempo hace?
It's hot.	Hace calor.
It's cold.	Hace frío.
It's windy.	Hace viento.
It's sunny.	Hace sol.
It's bad weather.	Hace mal tiempo.
It's good weather.	Hace buen tiempo.
It's snowing.	Está nevando.
It's raining.	Está lloviendo.
It's cloudy.	Está nublado.
It's partly cloudy.	Está medio nublado.
Rain	La lluvia
Snow	La nieve
There's a lot of rain/a lot of snow.	Hay mucha lluvia / mucha nieve.

IMPORTANT NOTE: When it's snowing or raining we just use the verb for "to snow" (nevar) or "to rain" (llover). In this case, we do not use "hace." Instead, we use the verb, "ESTAR" (to be). For example, "Está lloviendo/nevando." Or, "It is raining/snowing."

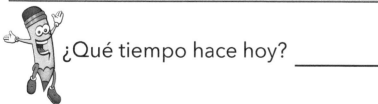 ¿Qué tiempo hace hoy? _____

ROLE PLAY – **"¿Qué tiempo hace?"**

Let's practice describing what the weather is like where you live during a certain season or month.

Scenario #1:

It is the middle of August and it's HOT outside.

Say in Spanish:

YOUR FRIEND: "¿Qué tiempo hace?"

YOU: "Hace sol y mucho calor."

Scenario #2:

It is the middle of February and it's snowing and cold outside.

Say in Spanish:

YOUR FRIEND: "¿Qué tiempo hace?"

YOU: "Hace frío y está nevando mucho."

Lesson Summary

I can say the days of the week in Spanish!

> Lunes, martes, miércoles, jueves, viernes, sábado, domingo.

I can say the months of the year in Spanish!

> Enero, febrero, marzo, abril, mayo, junio, Julio, agosto, septiembre, octubre, noviembre, diciembre.

I can say the seasons in Spanish!

> **El invierno** (winter), **la primavera** (spring), **el verano** (summer), **el otoño** (fall).

I can describe the weather in Spanish!

> Some of the most common ways to describe the weather in Spanish are: **"Hace calor."** (It's hot). **"Hace frío."** (It's cold.) **"Hace sol."** (It's sunny.) **"Hace viento."** (It's windy.) For rain and snow we say, **"Está nevando."** (It's snowing.) Or, **"Está lloviendo."** (It's raining.)

SPANISH CALENDAR & WEATHER

Fill in the chart below with the months by group that fall under each season. Use the word bank for help!

Group 1:
diciembre
enero
febrero

Group 2:
marzo
abril
mayo

Group 3:
septiembre
octubre
noviembre

Group 4:
junio
julio
agosto

VERANO	INVIERNO	OTOÑO	PRIMAVERA

Unscramble the days of the week! Below are the days of the week in Spanish but they are out of order. Put them in the correct order starting with Monday – Sunday. **(sábado, jueves, martes, viernes, domingo, lunes, miércoles)**

1. _____
2. _____
3. _____
4. _____
5. _____
6. _____
7. _____

Unscramble the months of the year! Now do the same thing with the months of the year. Put them in the correct order starting with January – December.

marzo   **febrero**   **diciembre**

noviembre   **julio**   **enero**

agosto   **junio**   **mayo**

septiembre   **octubre**   **abril**

1. _____   7. _____

2. _____   8. _____

3. _____   9. _____

4. _____   10 _____

5. _____   11. _____

6. _____   12. _____

¿Hace frío o hace calor? (Is it cold or hot?) Finish each sentence below using the phrase, "Hace frío." Or "Hace calor."

En verano… _____

En invierno… _____

En enero… _____

En diciembre… _____

En agosto… _____

En julio… _____

Hoy… _____

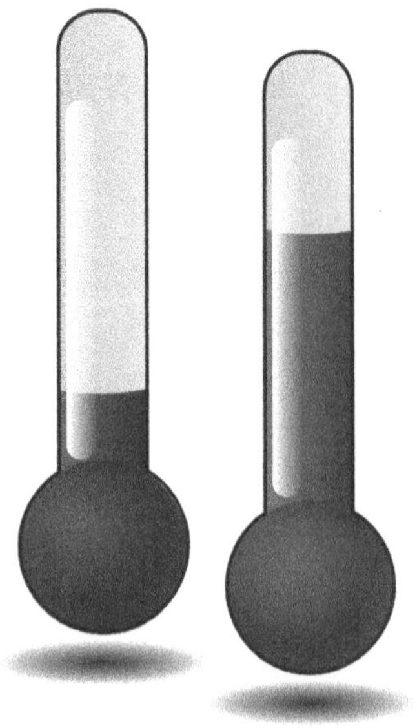

¿Qué tiempo hace?

What's the weather like? Answer the following questions referring to the weather forecast below. Refer to the examples for help!

Lunes	Martes	Miércoles	Jueves	Viernes	Sábado	Domingo

¿Hace calor el domingo?	*No, hace frío el domingo.*
¿Hace viento el miércoles?	*Sí, hace viento el miércoles.*
¿Qué tiempo hace el lunes?	
¿Nieva el domingo?	
¿Hace viento el jueves?	
¿Hace calor el martes?	
¿Hace sol el martes?	
¿Hace frío el domingo?	
¿Llueve el viernes?	
¿Qué día hace sol?	*Hace sol el martes.*
¿Qué día hace frío?	
¿Qué día hace viento?	
¿Qué día hace calor?	

¿Qué tiempo hace?

What's the weather like? Look at each picture and describe the weather in Spanish. Then, practice saying each sentence out loud to a friend.

_____

_____

_____

_____

_____

Lesson 4 – Telling Time, Definite Articles, & School Vocabulary

What will we learn in this lesson?

By the end of this lesson, you will be able to:
- Describe how "articles" are used with nouns
- Say the time in Spanish to the hour
- Say the time in Spanish to the quarter hour
- Say the time in Spanish to the half hour
- Say the time in Spanish to the minute
- Use common "telling time" vocabulary
- Conjugate the verb "IR" (to go) in the present tense
- Use common vocabulary related to school

Introduction to Definite Articles

What are "definite articles?" Definite articles are kind-of a fancy way of saying "THE" in Spanish. In English we use one word for "THE" and in Spanish, it's a little trickier.

There are four "articles." Why? Well, because in Spanish nouns are either masculine or feminine, singular or plural. Let's take a closer look!

EL   We use "EL" for nouns that are masculine, singular.

     EL GATO – the male cat

LOS   "LOS" is the plural of "EL" or masculine, plural.

     LOS GATOS – the male cats

LA   We use "LA" for nouns that are feminine, singular.

     LA GATA – the female cat

LAS   "LAS" is the plural of "LA" or feminine, plural.

     LAS GATAS – the female cats

"How do I know if a noun is masculine or feminine?"

It's not always easy to tell if a noun is masculine or feminine especially when we're talking about a non-living thing. Often, nouns that end in "o" are masculine, and nouns that end in "a" are feminine, but not all nouns end in "o" or "a" and not all nouns follow this rule! So, when you learn a new vocabulary word, you just have to learn the article with it! Don't worry, you'll get used to it!

¿Qué hora es? (What time is it?)

Telling time in Spanish is not difficult as long as you follow these simple rules. Time, as in time on a clock, in Spanish is called "LA HORA" or the hour. Don't confuse this with "EL TIEMPO" which actually refers to the weather or the passage of time, not the time of the day!

Let's break it down by telling time on the hour, quarter after the hour, half past the hour, and to the minute.

ON THE HOUR

For the hour of 1:00 we say "ES LA UNA."

"Es la una." – It's 1:00.

NOW YOU TRY!

For the hour of 2:00 – 12:00, we say "SON LAS" + (HOUR)

"Son las dos." – It's 2:00.

"Son las tres." – It's 3:00.

NOW YOU TRY!

QUARTER AFTER THE HOUR

When it's quarter past the hour, or 15 minutes after the hour, we simply add "y cuarto" to the time.

"Es la una y cuarto." – It's 1:15.

"Son las dos y cuarto." – It's 2:15.

NOW YOU TRY!

HALF PAST THE HOUR

When it's half past the hour, or 30 minutes after the hour, we simply add "y media" to the time.

"Es la una y media." – It's 1:30.

"Son las dos y media." – It's 2:30.

NOW YOU TRY!

TO THE MINUTE

To say what time it is to the minute, we simply add "Y" + (MINUTE)

"Es la una y cinco." – It's 1:05.

"Son las dos y diecisiete." – It's 2:17.

NOW YOU TRY!

Useful "Telling Time" Vocabulary

In the morning (a.m.)	De la mañana.
In the afternoon (before dark, p.m.)	De la tarde.
In the evening (after dark, p.m.)	De la noche.
The hour / an hour	La hora / una hora
The minute / a minute	El minuto / un minuto
The second / a second	El segundo / un segundo
The moment / a moment / a little moment	El momento / un momento / un momentito
A while. / In a while. / In a little while.	Un rato. / En un rato. / En un ratito.
Right away.	En seguida.
Now. / Right now.	Ahora. / Ahora mismo. / Ahorita.

IMPORTANT NOTE: When telling time in Spanish, you use "y" to describe past the hour, up to half past the hour. For example, it's 2:25. "Son las dos y veinticinco."

However, when you are past the half of the hour, you start to use "menos" in describing the time. For example, it's 20 minutes to 5. "Son las cinco menos veinte."

Introduction to "IR" (To Go)

The verb "IR" means "to go" in Spanish. We use IR to describe where we are going or what we are going to do. Let's learn how to conjugate this important verb in the present tense!

I go	Yo **VOY**
You go	Tú **VAS**
He / She / You (formal) goes/go	Él / Ella / Usted (Ud.) **VA**
We go	Nosotros/as **VAMOS**
You all (informal) go	Vosotros/as **VAIS**
They / You all (formal) go	Ellos / Ellas / Ustedes (Uds.) **VAN**

¿A qué hora? (At what time?)

In Spanish, when we want to know at what time something is going to happen, we say: "¿A qué hora?" (At what time?)

For example:

At what time do you go to school? – "¿A qué hora vas a la escuela?"

I go to school at 9:00. – "Voy a la escuela a las nueve."

IMPORTANT NOTE: When saying "to the," remember the following:

a + el = al... (al parque – to the park)

a + la = a la... (a la escuela – to the school)

Vocabulario Nuevo (New Vocabulary)

Schedule	El horario
Class	La clase
School	La escuela
Library	La biblioteca
Home/house	La casa
Park	El parque
Dentist	El dentista
Movie theatre	El cine

PRACTICE

Using the information below, answer the following questions about your schedule.

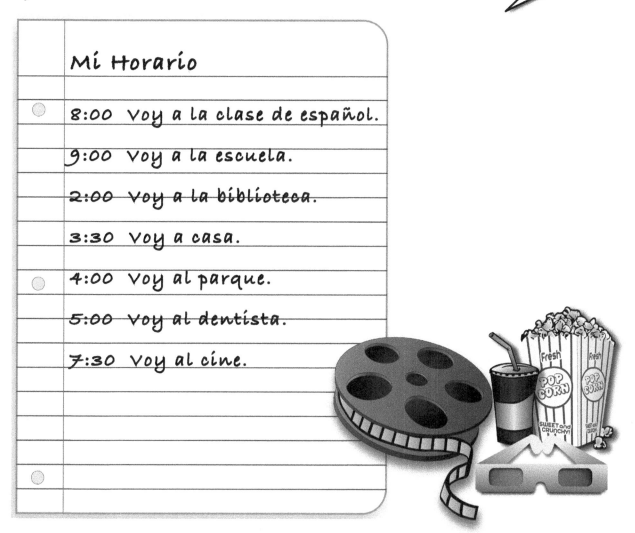

Mi Horario

8:00 Voy a la clase de español.

9:00 Voy a la escuela.

2:00 Voy a la biblioteca.

3:30 Voy a casa.

4:00 Voy al parque.

5:00 Voy al dentista.

7:30 Voy al cine.

1. ¿A qué hora vas al dentista? - "Voy al dentista a las cinco."

2. ¿A qué hora vas a casa?

3. ¿A qué hora vas al parque?

4. ¿A qué hora vas al cine?

5. ¿A qué hora vas a la biblioteca?

6. ¿A qué hora vas a la clase de español?

7. ¿A qué hora vas a la escuela?

Vocabulario de la Escuela (School Vocabulary)

School	La escuela
Lunch	El almuerzo
Recess	El recreo
Schedule	El horario
Homework	La tarea
Teacher	El maestro / la maestra
Student	El estudiante / la estudiante
Desk (student)	El pupitre
Desk (teacher)	El escritorio
Computer	La computadora
Table	La mesa
Chair	La silla
Pencil	El lápiz
Pen	El bolígrafo / la pluma
Window	La ventana
Paper	El papel
Eraser	La goma de borrar / el borrador
Glue	El pegamento
Ruler	La regla
Crayons	Los crayones
Scissors	Las tijeras
Notebook	El cuaderno
Folder	La carpeta
Book	El libro
Backpack	La mochila
Classroom	La sala de clase

¿Qué tienes en tu mochila? (What do you have in your backpack?)

_____

Lesson Summary

I know how to use articles!

> There are four articles used with nouns: 1) **"EL"** – for nouns that are masculine, singular. 2) **"LOS"** – for nouns that are masculine, plural. 3) **"LA"** – for nouns that are feminine, plural. 4) **"LAS"** – for nouns that are feminine, plural.

I know how to say the time in Spanish on the hour!

> For the hour of 1:00, we say **"Es la una."** For 2:00 and later, we say **"Son las dos," "Son las tres,"** and so on.

I know how to say the time in Spanish to the quarter hour!

> When it's quarter past the hour, or 15 minutes after the hour, we simply add **"Y CUARTO"** to the time.

I know how to say the time in Spanish to the half hour!

> When it's half past the hour, or 30 minutes after the hour, we simply add **"Y MEDIA"** to the time.

I know how to say the time in Spanish to the minute!

> To say what time it is to the minute, we simply add **"Y"** + **(MINUTE)**.

I know how to use common "telling time" vocabulary!

> I know how to use common "telling time" vocabulary like, **"de la mañana"** (in the morning) or **"de la tarde"** (in the afternoon), and **"de la noche"** (in the evening).

I know how to conjugate the verb "IR" in the present tense!

> **Yo VOY** (I go), **Tú VAS** (you go), **Él/Ella/Usted VA** (he/she goes, you go), **Nosotros/as VAMOS** (we go), **Vosotros/as VAIS** (you all go), **Ellos/Ellas/Ustedes VAN** (they/you all go).

I know how to use common vocabulary related to school!

SCHOOL VOCABULARY CROSSWORD PUZZLE

ACROSS		DOWN	
1. La sala de …	12. Window	1. Computer	9. Pen
2. Teacher's desk	13. Backpack	2. Student	10. Lunch
3. Table	14. Chair	5. Homework	11. Student Desk
4. Pencil	15. Book	6. Folder	
8. Notebook	16. Recess	7. School	

"¿A qué hora vas?"

What time are you going? Look at the following schedule and then answer the questions below. Follow the examples.

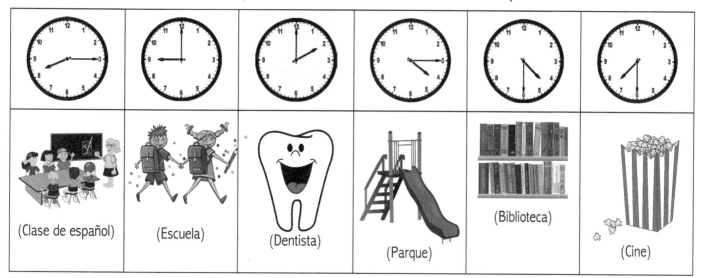

| (Clase de español) | (Escuela) | (Dentista) | (Parque) | (Biblioteca) | (Cine) |

1. ¿A qué hora vas a la clase de español?   *Voy a la clase de español a las ocho y cuarto.*

2. ¿A qué hora vas a la escuela?

3. ¿A qué hora vas al dentista?

4. ¿A qué hora vas al parque?

5. ¿A qué hora vas a la biblioteca?

6. ¿A qué hora vas al cine?

7. ¿Adónde vas a las dos?   *Voy al dentista a las dos.*

8. ¿Adónde vas a las ocho y cuarto?

9. ¿Adónde vas a las cuatro y media?

10. ¿Adónde vas a las siete y media?

Lesson 5 – Common Verbs & "Me Gusta"

What will we learn in this lesson?

By the end of this lesson, you will be able to:
- Say several common Spanish verbs
- Use vocabulary related to these verbs
- Use the phrase "Me gusta…" to describe what you like to do
- Use the phrase "No me gusta…" to describe what you don't like to do

Common Verbs

Like in English, verbs describe an action such as to run, to walk, to eat, etc. In Spanish, we call these verbs "infinitives," which means they are verbs that are not yet conjugated. To conjugate a verb means to use it in reference to the person taking the action. We'll talk more about verb conjugation in future lessons.

All Spanish verbs end in AR, ER, or IR. Just like with all new vocabulary, we have to start by memorizing it.

To use	Usar
To touch, to play an instrument	Tocar
To run	Correr
To read	Leer
To speak, to talk	Hablar
To write	Escribir
To swim	Nadar
To practice	Practicar
To see	Ver
To study	Estudiar
To dance	Bailar
To listen	Escuchar

To skate	Patinar
To sing	Cantar
To play	Jugar
To draw	Dibujar
To eat	Comer
To ride (a bike)	Montar (en bicicleta)
To ski	Esquiar
To do, to make	Hacer
To sleep	Dormir

REMINDER: All Spanish verbs, or infinitives, end in either "ER", "IR", or "AR." When we use the infinitive of a verb in Spanish, we are using the verb without conjugating it. For example, "correr" (to run), "caminar" (to walk), or escribir (to write).

More Useful Vocabulary

Music	La música
Television	La tele
Sports	Los deportes
Guitar	La guitarra
Videogames	Los videojuegos
Bicycle	La bicicleta
Radio	La radio
Soccer / to play soccer	El fútbol / jugar al fútbol
Telephone / to talk on the phone	El teléfono / hablar por teléfono

"¿Te gusta ver la tele?"

¿Qué te gusta hacer? (What do you like to do?)

Now that we know a bunch of verbs, let's learn how to talk about what we like to do, and what we don't like to do! Here's the formula for saying what you like to do, or what you don't like to do:

"ME GUSTA" + (VERB) = "I LIKE TO (VERB)"
"Me gusta bailar." (I like to dance.)
"Me gusta nadar." (I like to swim.)

"NO ME GUSTA" + (VERB) = "I DON'T LIKE TO (VERB)"
"No me gusta estudiar." (I don't like to study.)
"No me gusta cantar." (I don't like to sing.)

"TE GUSTA" + (VERB) = "YOU LIKE TO (VERB)"
"Te gusta bailar." (You like to dance.)
"Te gusta nadar." (You like to swim.)

"NO TE GUSTA" + (VERB) = "YOU DON'T LIKE TO (VERB)"
"No te gusta estudiar." (You don't like to study.)
"No te gusta cantar." (You don't like to sing.)

A ELLA LE GUSTA" + (VERB) = "SHE LIKES TO (VERB)"
A ÉL LE GUSTA" + (VERB) = "HE LIKES TO (VERB)"
"A ella le gusta estudiar." (She likes to study.)
"A él le gusta nadar." (He likes to swim.)

NOW YOU TRY!

¿Te gusta...? (Do you like...?) Some common answers to this question might be:

Yes / No	Sí / No
Very much / very, very much	Mucho / muchísimo
Me too.	A mí también.
Me neither.	A mí tampoco.

PRACTICE

Walk around the room and ask other students in Spanish what they like to do. Put a check mark under the "¡Sí, me gusta mucho!" column or under the "¡No, no me gusta nada!" column depending on each student's answer.

¿Te gusta...?	¡Sí, me gusta mucho!	¡No, no me gusta nada!
Estudiar?		
Bailar?		
Cantar?		
Leer?		
Nadar?		
Patinar?		
Escuchar música?		
Ver la tele?		
Jugar videojuegos?		
Dibujar?		
Montar en bicicleta?		

Lesson Summary

I know how to say some common Spanish verbs!

I know the following verbs: **USAR** (to use), **TOCAR** (to touch, to play an instrument), **CORRER** (to run), **LEER** (to read), **HABLAR** (to speak), **ESCRIBIR** (to write), **NADAR** (to swim), **PRACTICAR** (to practice), **VER** (to see), **ESTUDIAR** (to study), **BAILAR** (to dance), **ESCUCHAR** (to listen), **PATINAR** (to skate), **CANTAR** (to sing), **JUGAR** (to play), **DIBUJAR** (to draw), **MONTAR** (to ride), **COMER** (to eat), **ESQUIAR** (to ski), **HACER** (to make, to do), **DORMIR** (to sleep).

I know more useful vocabulary often used with these verbs!

I know how to use the phrase "Me gusta…" to describe what I like to do!

To say what I like to do, I use, **"ME GUSTA + (VERB)."**

I know how to use the phrase "No me gusta…" to describe what I don't like to do!

To say what I don't like to do, I use, **"NO ME GUSTA + (VERB)."**

¡VERBOS, VERBOS, VERBOS!

Label each picture with the correct Spanish verb infinitive from the word bank below.

Nadar	Cantar	Ver la tele
Bailar	Dormir	Correr
Dibujar	Comer	Tocar la guitarra
Esquiar	Hablar por teléfono	Leer
Estudiar	Jugar al fútbol	Montar en bicicleta

"¿Qué te gusta hacer?"

What do you like to do? Answer each of the following questions using a complete sentence. You must answer some questions "yes" and some questions "no." Follow the example.

1. ¿Te gusta montar en bicicleta?

Sí, me gusta montar en bicicleta. / No, no me gusta montar en bicicleta.

2. ¿Te gusta cantar?

_____

3. ¿Te gusta leer libros?

_____

4. ¿Te gusta comer?

_____

5. ¿Te gusta ver la tele?

_____

6. ¿Te gusta bailar?

_____

7. ¿Te gusta hablar por teléfono?

_____

8. ¿Te gusta nadar?

_____

9. ¿Te gusta dibujar?

_____

1o. ¿Te gusta escuchar música?

_____

11. ¿Te gusta estudiar?

_____

Lesson 6 – The Body, "Me Duele" & Introduction to Animals

What will we learn in this lesson?

By the end of this lesson, you will be able to:
- Name common parts of the body in Spanish
- Use the phrase "Me duele…" with parts of the body when describing what hurts
- Name common animals of the farm
- Name common animals of the ocean
- Name common animals of the jungle

The Body (El Cuerpo)

Nose	La nariz		
Head	La cabeza		
Knee	La rodilla		
Leg	La pierna		
Foot	El pie		
Back	La espalda	Heart	El corazón
Eye	El ojo	Shoulders	Los hombros
Hand	La mano	Ear	La oreja
Finger	El dedo	Neck	El cuello
Elbow	El codo	Throat	La garganta
Stomach	El estómago	Teeth	Los dientes
Mouth	La boca	Tongue	La lengua
Hair	El pelo	Arm	El brazo

NOTE: Notice the Spanish word for hand or "la mano" is feminine! This one is tricky, but common, so remember!

Using "Me duele..."

In Spanish when we want to describe a part of our body that hurts, we use the phrase "Me duele" meaning that something "hurts me." For example, to say that your arm hurts in Spanish you would say, "Me duele el brazo."

Here's the simple formula:

> ME DUELE + ARTICLE (el or la) + BODY PART
>
> "Me duele el dedo." – My finger hurts.
>
> "Me duele la garganta." – My throat hurts.

NOW YOU TRY!

To ask a friend if his/her body hurts, we change the formula by adding "TE" like this:

> TE DUELE + ARTICLE (el or la) + BODY PART
>
> "¿Te duele el dedo?" – Does your finger hurt?
>
> "¿Te duele la garganta?" – Does your throat hurt?

NOW YOU TRY!

Some responses might be:

Yes, a lot. / Yes, very much!	Sí, mucho. / ¡Sí, muchísimo!
No, not very much.	No, no mucho.
A ton!	¡Un montón!

> **IMPORTANT NOTE:** When using "me duele…" and you are talking about more than one part of your body that hurts, you say, "Me duelen…" For example, my feet hurt. – "Me duelen los piés." My head and my throat hurt. – "Me duelen la cabeza y la garganta."

PRACTICE

Sit down with a friend and ask him or her the following questions.

- ¿Te duele la cabeza?
- ¿Te duele el estómago?
- ¿Te duele la espalda?
- ¿Te duele la garganta?

Los Animales de la Granja (Animals of the Farm)

Farm	La granja
Dog	El perro
Cat	El gato
Cow	La vaca
Rooster	El gallo
Duck	El pato
Donkey	El burro
Chick	El pollito
Horse	El caballo
Sheep	La oveja
Pig	El cerdo
Mouse	El ratón
Bird	El pájaro

Los Animales del Océano (Animals of the Ocean)

Ocean / sea	El océano / el mar
Shark	El tiburón
Seal	La foca
Whale	La ballena
Fish	El pez
Crab	El cangrejo
Lobster	La langosta
Dolphin	El delfín
Star fish	La estrella de mar
Octopus	El pulpo

Los Animales de la Selva (Animals of the Jungle)

Jungle	La jungla / la selva
Puma	El puma
Monkey	El mono
Parrot	El loro

Frog	La rana
Elephant	El elefante
Turtle	La tortuga
Lion	El león
Tiger	El tigre
Giraffe	La jirafa
Zebra	La cebra

¿Cual es tu animal favorito? (What is your favorite animal?)

EXAMPLE: "Mi animal favorito es el perro." (My favorite animal is the dog.)

Lesson Summary

I can name common parts of the body in Spanish!

El ojo, la nariz, la cabeza, la rodilla, la pierna, el pie, la espalda, la mano, el dedo, el codo, el estómago, la boca, el pelo, la oreja, el brazo, el cuello, la garganta, los dientes, la lengua.

I can use the phrase "Me duele..." to describe a part of my body that hurts in Spanish! It's simple: **ME DUELE + ARTICLE (el or la) + BODY PART**

I can name common animals of the farm in Spanish!

El perro, el gato, la vaca, el gallo, el pato, el burro, el pollito, el caballo, la oveja, el ratón, el pájaro.

I can name common animals of the ocean in Spanish!

La ballena, la foca, el tiburón, el delfín, el cangrejo, la langosta, el pez, la estrella de mar, el pulpo.

I can name common animals of the jungle in Spanish!

El puma, el mono, el loro, la rana, el elefante, la tortuga, el león, el tigre, la jirafa, la cebra.

"¿Qué le duele?"

What hurts? Look at the picture and answer the question, "¿Qué le duele?" (Follow the example.)

LA COLA

"Le duele la cola."

_____

LA CABEZA

_____

EL CUERPO

_____

EL BRAZO

_____

EL CORAZÓN

_____

LA PIERNA

_____

NAME THE FARM ANIMALS

Write the name of the animal next to its picture in Spanish and don't forget the article. Use the word bank to help!

El perro   El gallo   El pollito   El ratón

El gato   El pato   El caballo   El pájaro

La vaca   El burro   La oveja   El cerdo

NAME THE OCEAN ANIMALS

Write the name of the animal next to its picture in Spanish and don't forget the article. Use the word bank to help!

La ballena   El cangrejo   El delfín

La foca   La langosta   El pulpo

El pez   El tiburón   La estrella de mar

NAME THE JUNGLE ANIMALS

Write the name of the animal next to its picture in Spanish and don't forget the article. Use the word bank to help!

El mono   El elefante   El tigre

El loro   La tortuga   La jirafa

La rana   El león   La cebra

LAS PARTES DEL CUERPO

Label the names of the parts of the body in Spanish as indicated in the chart below. Then, color the pictures.

LA CHICA

El pelo	La nariz
El brazo	Las piernas
El cuello	Los dedos
La espalda	Las rodillas

EL CHICO

La boca	Las orejas
Los pies	Los ojos
El estómago	La mano
El codo	Los hombros

PREGUNTAS DE LA LECCIÓN

Circle the correct answers to the following questions from the lesson. Note that more than one answer may be correct.

1. ¿Cuáles son los animales de la granja?

El caballo   La oveja   La rana

La ballena   El loro   La vaca

2. ¿Cuáles son los animales del océano?

El tiburón   La foca   La cebra

El gato   El pollito   El pez

3. ¿Cuáles son los animales de la selva?

El mono   El pulpo   La jirafa

El perro   La estrella de mar   El puma

4. Circle the parts on the body that hurt these kids.

- A él le duelen la cabeza, la garganta, y el estómago.

- A ella le duelen las piernas, los brazos, y las manos.

Lesson 7 – Asking Questions, Adjectives, & My Family

What will we learn in this lesson?

By the end of this lesson, you will be able to:

- Use "asking questions" vocabulary
- Use common adjectives to describe yourself and others
- Name the members of your family in Spanish
- Use common phrases to describe yourself and others

Review of the verb SER

The verb "SER" means "to be" in Spanish. One important way that we use SER is with adjectives to describe ourselves and others. Let's review how to conjugate this important verb in the present tense!

I am	Yo **SOY**
You are	Tú **ERES**
He / She / You (formal) are	Él / Ella / Usted (Ud.) **ES**
We are	Nosotros/as **SOMOS**
You all (informal) are	Vosotros/as **SOIS**
They / You all (formal) are	Ellos / Ellas / Ustedes (Uds.) **SON**

Asking Questions Vocabulary

Who?	¿Quién?
Why?	¿Por qué?
What?	¿Qué?
When?	¿Cuándo?
Where?	¿Dónde?
To where?	¿Adónde?

How?	¿Cómo?
How many?	¿Cuántos?
How much?	¿Cuánto?
Which?	¿Cuál?
Which ones?	¿Cuáles?

Using Adjectives

Just like in English, we use adjectives to describe nouns. In Spanish, when we use adjectives, we need to remember to make sure the adjective "agrees" with the noun, meaning whether or not the noun is feminine or masculine, singular or plural. When describing people, it's easy. If you're talking about a girl, it's feminine and if you're talking about a boy, it's masculine.

For example,

"Él es reservado." – Meaning, "He is shy."

"Ella es reservada." – Meaning, "She is shy."

Common Spanish Adjectives

Neat, organized	Ordenado/a		
Patient	Paciente		
Fun	Divertido/a		
Studious	Estudioso/a		
Interesting	Interesante		
Impatient	Impaciente		
Difficult	Difícil	Hardworking	Trabajador/a
Lazy	Perezoso/a	Sociable	Sociable
Daring	Atrevido/a	Funny	Gracioso/a
Athletic	Deportista	Messy	Desordenado/a
Independent	Independiente	Nice, friendly	Simpático/a
Reserved, shy	Reservado/a	Artistic	Artístico/a
Well-liked	Popular	Talented	Talentoso/a
Good	Bueno/a	Not nice, mean	Antipático
Intelligent/smart	Inteligente	Serious	Serio/a

Mi Familia (My Family)

Family	La familia
Father / Mother	El padre / la madre
Parents	Los padres
Dad / mom	El papá / la mamá
Brother / sister	El hermano / la hermana
Son / daughter	El hijo / la hija
Children	Los hijos
Grandfather / grandmother	El abuelo / la abuela
Grandson / granddaughter	El nieto / la nieta
Uncle / aunt	El tío / la tía
Nephew / niece	El sobrino / la sobrina
Cousin	El primo / la prima
Pet	La mascota
Dog	El perro
Cat	El gato

PRACTICE

Drill #1:

Tell us about the people in your family! Let's answer some common questions about your family. In some cases, be sure to use the adjectives you just learned!

¿Cómo se llaman tus padres? – "Mis padres se llaman…"

¿Cuántas personas hay en tu familia? – "Hay…personas en mi familia."

¿Cuántos hijos hay en tu familia? – "Hay…hijos en mi familia."

¿Cómo se llaman tus hermanos? – "Mis hermanos se llaman…"

¿Cuántos primos tienes? – "Tengo…primos."

¿Cómo se llaman tus primos? – "Mis primos se llaman…"

¿Cómo es tu padre? – "Mi padre es…"

¿Cómo es tu madre? – "Mi madre es…"

¿Cómo es tu hermano o tu hermana? – "Mi hermano/hermana es…"

¿Cuántos abuelos tienes? – "Tengo…abuelos."

¿Tienes mascota? - "Sí, tengo mascota." "No, no tengo mascota."

¿Cómo se llama tu mascota? – "Mi mascota se llama…"

Drill #2:

Using your new list of adjectives, tell us a little about yourself. What are you like? What are you not like?

Lesson Summary

I know how to use "asking questions" vocabulary!

> **¿Quién?** (who), **¿Por qué?** (why), **¿Qué?** (what), **¿Cuándo?** (when), **¿Dónde?** (where), **¿Adónde?** (to where), **¿Cómo?** (how), **¿Cuántos?** (how many), **¿Cuánto?** (how much), **¿Cuál?** (which), **¿Cuáles?** (which ones).

I know to use common adjectives to describe myself and others!

I can name the members of my family!

> **Padre / madre / padres** (father / mother / parents), **papá / mamá** (dad / mom), **hermano/a** (brother / sister), **hijo/a / hijos** (son / daughter / children), **abuelo/a** (grandpa / grandma), **nieto/a** (grandson / granddaughter), **sobrino/a** (nephew / niece), **primo/a** (cousin), **mascota / perro / gato** (pet / dog / cat), **familia** (family).

I can use common phrases to describe myself and others!

COMPREHENSION EXERCISE

DIRECTIONS: Read the following paragraph and answer the questions below.

"Yo tengo una familia muy grande y vivimos en una casa muy pequeña. Tengo tres hermanos, dos hermanas, y tengo cuatro mascotas. Tengo un gato que se llama Frisky, un perro que se llama Tico, un loro que se llama Polly, y una rana que se llama Felix. Hoy vamos al veterinario porque a mi rana le duele la pierna."

Questions:

1. ¿Cómo es la familia?
2. ¿Cuántos hermanos tiene?
3. ¿Cuántas hermanas tiene?
4. ¿Cuántas mascotas tiene?
5. ¿Cómo se llama el perro?
6. ¿Cómo se llama el gato?
7. ¿Cómo se llama el loro?
8. ¿Cómo se llama la rana?
9. ¿Qué le duele a la rana?
10. ¿Es la casa grande o pequeña?

New Vocabulary:

Veterinarian	El veterinario
House	La casa
I have…	(Yo) tengo…
We live…	Vivimos…
Large / small	Grande / pequeña

QUESTIONS & ADJECTIVES REVIEW

1. Write the correct letter next to each question word!

☐	Which ones?	a. ¿Quién?
☐	What?	b. ¿Cuáles?
☐	Where?	c. ¿Cuántos?
☐	Why?	d. ¿Por qué?
☐	How?	e. ¿Qué?
☐	Which?	f. ¿Dónde?
☐	How much?	g. ¿Cuánto?
☐	To where?	h. ¿Cuándo?
☐	How many?	i. ¿Cómo?
☐	When?	j. ¿Adónde?
☐	Who?	k. ¿Cuál?

2. El hijo de mi papá es mi_____? (circle one)

- Primo
- Abuelo
- Hermano
- Hija

3. La hermana de mi mamá es mi _____? (circle one)

- Hermana
- Prima
- Hija
- Tía

4. La mamá de mi padre es mi_____? (circle one)

- Sobrina
- Abuela
- Hermana
- Prima

5. Los hijos de mis tíos son mis_____? (circle one)

- Primos
- Hijos
- Sobrinos
- Padres

6. La madre de mi mamá es mi_____? (circle one)

- Tía
- Hermana
- Abuela
- Prima

7. Mi hermano es el_____ de mi abuela. (circle one)

- Primo
- Nieto
- Hijo
- Sobrino

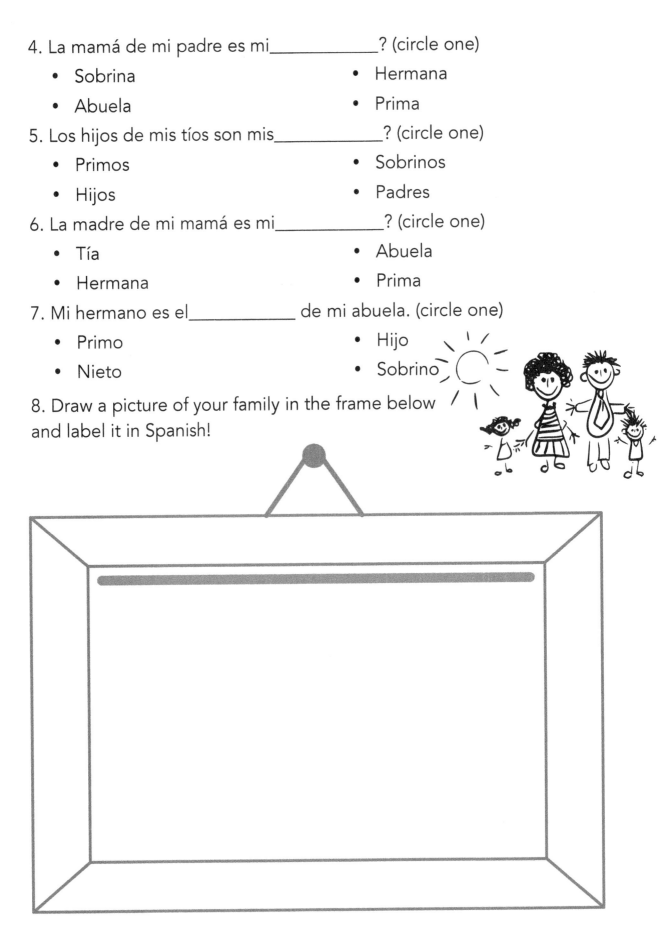

8. Draw a picture of your family in the frame below and label it in Spanish!

8. Look at the pictures. Write under each picture an adjective in Spanish that would describe each person. (Use the word bank.)

Inteligente   Ordenada   Perezoso

Estudiosa   Atrevido   Reservado

Deportista   Artístico   Simpáticos

¿CÓMO ES?

What is he/she like? Read each sentence in Spanish and then answer the question, ¿Cómo es él? or, ¿Cómo es ella? Use one Spanish adjective from the word bank that is the most fitting for each question.

Simpática   Reservada   Sociable

Estudiosa   Deportista   Trabajador

Perezoso   Atrevido   Ordenada

1. A mi hermano le gusta mucho ver la tele y dormir. ¿Cómo es él? _____

2. A mi hermana le gusta mucho hablar por teléfono con sus amigas. ¿Cómo es ella? _____

3. A mi padre le gusta mucho trabajar. ¿Cómo es él? _____

4. A mi prima no le gusta hablar con la gente (people). ¿Cómo es ella? _____

5. A mi mamá le gusta mucho una casa limpia (clean house). ¿Cómo es ella? _____

6. A mi primo le gusta mucho jugar al fútbol y correr. ¿Cómo es él? _____

7. A mi amiga le gusta mucho estudiar y hacer (to do) la tarea. ¿Cómo es ella? _____

8. A mi tía le gusta mucho la gente. ¿Cómo es ella? _____

9. A mi abuelo le gusta mucho esquiar en las montañas. ¿Cómo es él? _____

Lesson 8 – Food & Introduction to the Present Tense

What will we learn in this lesson?

By the end of this lesson, you will be able to:

- Conjugate regular Spanish verbs in the present tense
- Explain what the "infinitive" form of a verb is
- Explain what an "irregular" verb is
- Use common Spanish food vocabulary
- Speak in the present tense in Spanish!

The Present Tense – Regular Verbs

To speak in the present tense in Spanish with all regular verbs, the formula is easy! You take the verb in its infinitive, remove the AR/ER/IR ending, and replace it with the proper ending that corresponds to the person, or pronoun, taking the action.

But what is the present tense? In general, the present tense refers to an action that is taking place in the "present." Examples are: I eat, you sing, we dance, they run, etc.

Remember, all Spanish verbs end with AR, ER, or IR. This is called the infinitive of the verb, or a verb that is not conjugated. For example, COMER (to eat), TOMAR (to take or to drink), or VIVIR (to live).

Look at the chart below to see how we conjugate all regular Spanish verbs in the present tense.

PRONOUNS	AR VERBS	ER VERBS	IR VERBS
Yo	O	O	O
Tú	AS	ES	ES
Él / Ella / Usted	A	E	E
Nosotros/as	AMOS	EMOS	IMOS
Ellos/as / Ustedes	AN	EN	EN

When speaking in the present tense in Spanish, conjugate regular verbs by using this simple formula:

1. **TAKE** THE VERB INFINITIVE

2. **REMOVE** "AR/ER/IR"

3. **REPLACE** WITH THE PROPER ENDING

Let's try this formula with the following verbs: COMER, TOMAR and VIVIR.

PERSON	INFINITIVE	NEW ENDING
I - **YO**	TO EAT - COM**ER**	I EAT - YO COM**O**
I - **YO**	TO DRINK - TOM**AR**	I DRINK - YO TOM**O**
I - **YO**	TO LIVE - VIV**IR**	I LIVE - YO VIV**O**
YOU - **TÚ**	TO EAT - COM**ER**	YOU EAT - TÚ COM**ES**
YOU – **TÚ**	TO DRINK - TOM**AR**	YOU DRINK - TÚ TOM**AS**
YOU – **TÚ**	TO LIVE - VIV**IR**	YOU LIVE - TÚ VIV**ES**
SHE - **ELLA**	TO EAT - COM**ER**	SHE EATS - ELLA COM**E**
SHE - **ELLA**	TO DRINK - TOM**AR**	SHE DRINKS - ELLA TOM**A**
SHE - **ELLA**	TO LIVE - VIV**IR**	SHE LIVES - ELLA VIV**E**

Okay, so I know what a REGULAR Spanish verb is and how to conjugate it in the present tense, but what's an IRREGULAR Spanish verb? An IRREGULAR Spanish verb is a verb that doesn't follow the formula. You simply have to learn how to conjugate these verbs separately. An example of an irregular verb you already know is SER (to be).

Remember this?

I am	Yo **SOY**
You are	Tú **ERES**
He / She / You (formal) are	Él / Ella / Usted **ES**
We are	Nosotros/as **SOMOS**
They / You all (formal) are	Ellos / Ellas / Ustedes (Uds.) **SON**

Vocabulario de "La Comida" (Food Vocabulary)

¡Me gusta comer! (I like to eat!) Everyone has a favorite food so let's take a look at the following food-related vocabulary in Spanish. First, let's start with the names of the three main meals and then we'll look at some other useful Spanish vocabulary related to eating and meals.

The three main meals are:

- El desayuno (breakfast)
- El almuerzo (lunch)
- La cena (dinner)

El Desayuno (Breakfast)

Eggs	Los huevos
Pancakes	Los panqueques
Oatmeal	La avena
Bacon	El tocino
Cereal	El cereal
Yogurt	El yogur

El Almuerzo (Lunch)

Hamburger	La hamburguesa
Hot dog	El perrito caliente
French fries	Las papas fritas
Sandwich	El sandwich
Soup	La sopa

La Cena (Dinner)

Chicken	El pollo
Steak	El bistec
Fish	El pescado
Rice	El arroz
Bread	El pan

Salad	La ensalada
Pizza	La pizza
Spaghetti	El espagueti

Los Cubiertos (Place-Setting)

Fork	El tenedor
Knife	El cuchillo
Spoon	La cuchara
Napkin	La servilleta
Plate	El plato
Glass	El vaso

Las Bebidas (Drinks)

Milk	La leche
Tea	El té
Coffee	El café
Juice	El jugo
Water	El agua
Soft drink	El refresco

Las Frutas y Las Verduras (Fruits & Vegetables)

Bananas	Los plátanos
Strawberries	Las fresas
Apple	La manzana
Watermelon	La sandía
Orange	La naranja
Pear	La pera
Grapes	Las uvas
Carrot	La zanahoria
Tomato	El tomate
Potato	La patata
Onion	La cebolla

El Postre (Dessert)

Ice cream	El helado
Cookies	Las galletas
Candy	Los dulces
Donut	La rosquilla
Cake	El pastel

More Verbs!

To eat	Comer
To drink	Beber
To take or to drink	Tomar
To eat breakfast	Desayunar
To eat lunch	Almorzar
To eat dinner	Cenar
To live	Vivir

PRACTICE

Sit down with a friend and ask him or her the following questions:

- ¿Cuál es tu bebida favorita?
- ¿Cuál es tu desayuno favorito?
- ¿Cuál es tu almuerzo favorito?
- ¿Cuál es tu cena favorita?
- ¿Cuál es tu postre favorito?
- ¿Cuál es tu fruta y verdura favorita?

Lesson Summary

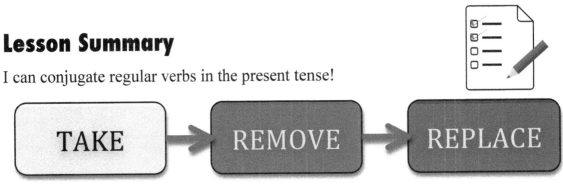

I can conjugate regular verbs in the present tense!

1. **TAKE** THE VERB INFINITIVE

2. **REMOVE** "AR/ER/IR"

3. **REPLACE** WITH THE PROPER ENDING

I can explain what the "infinitive" form of a verb is!

> The infinitive form of all Spanish verbs end in **AR**, **ER**, or **IR**. These are verbs that have not yet be conjugated like, **COMER** (to eat), **TOMAR** (to take or to drink), or **VIVIR** (to live).

I can explain what an "irregular" verb is!

> An "irregular" Spanish verb is one that doesn't follow the formula. You have to learn how to conjugate it differently. An example of an irregular Spanish verb is **SER** (to be).

I can use common Spanish food vocabulary!

I can speak in the present tense in Spanish!

PRONOUNS	AR VERBS	ER VERBS	IR VERBS
Yo	O	O	O
Tú	AS	ES	ES
Él / Ella / Usted	A	E	E
Nosotros/as	AMOS	EMOS	IMOS
Ellos/as / Ustedes	AN	EN	EN

¿Cuál es tu comida favorita?

What is your favorite meal? First, label the place setting below, (fork, knife, spoon, plate, glass, and napkin). Then, draw a picture of your favorite meal and label it in Spanish! Make sure to include at least one of each of the following:

- A main entrée (breakfast, lunch, or dinner)
- A fruit or a vegetable
- A drink

"LA COMIDA" CROSSWORD PUZZLE

ACROSS		DOWN	
5. To eat	14. Food	1. Hot Dog	8. To take or drink
6. Hamburger	15. Dinner	2. Water	9. Juice
7. Milk	16. Ice cream	3. Soup	12. Breakfast
8. Tea	17. Ham & cheese …	4. To drink	18. Coffee
10. To live	18. To eat dinner	6. Eggs	
11. Bacon	19. You eat it in a bowl		
13. Lunch	with milk for breakfast		

FOOD & PRESENT TENSE REVIEW

1. Circle all the verbs below that are in the INFINITIVE form of the verb. (HINT: You don't have to know what the verb means to know whether or not it's in the infinitive form of the verb!)

SER	TOMAR
BEBO	VIVIR
COMER	PASAMOS
COMEMOS	ESCUCHAR
JUGAR	USAR

2. What is the formula for conjugating regular verbs in the present tense?

3. Food questions - ¿Cierto o Falso? (True or False)
Write "CIERTO" or "FALSO" next to the following statements:

Yo como un perrito caliente para desayuno. _____

Mi mamá bebe café con desayuno. _____

Yo como helado para la cena. _____

Mi papá come tocino con huevos. _____

Yo bebo agua todos los días. _____

Yo como leche con el cereal. _____

Mi hermana come huevos para la cena. _____

THE PRESENT TENSE

Fill in the missing conjugated verbs. Then, translate the sentences below into Spanish.

PERSONAL PRONOUN	AR	TOMAR (to drink or to take)	ER	COMER (to eat)	IR	VIVIR (to live)
Yo	O	TOMO	O		O	
Tú	AS		ES	COMES	ES	
Él, Ella, Usted	A		E		E	
Nosotros/as	AMOS	TOMAMOS	EMOS		IMOS	
Ellos, Ellas, Ustedes	AN		EN		EN	

I drink. _____

We drink. _____

They drink. _____

You eat. _____

She eats. _____

We eat. _____

They live. _____

You all live. _____

THE PRESENT TENSE

Fill in the missing conjugated verbs. Then, translate the sentences below into Spanish.

PERSONAL PRONOUN	AR	CENAR (to eat dinner)	ER	BEBER (to drink)	IR	ESCRIBIR (to write)
Yo	O		O	BEBO	O	
Tú	AS	CENAS	ES		ES	
Él, Ella, Usted	A		E	BEBES	E	
Nosotros/as	AMOS		EMOS		IMOS	ESCRIBIMOS
Ellos, Ellas, Ustedes	AN		EN		EN	

I eat dinner. _____

We eat dinner. _____

They eat dinner. _____

You write. _____

He writes. _____

We write. _____

They drink. _____

You all drink. _____

Lesson 9 – Introduction to the Simple Future

What will we learn in this lesson?

By the end of this lesson, you will be able to:

- Conjugate the verb IR (to go) in the present tense
- Use the verb IR to speak in the simple future
- Use common vocabulary related to location
- Use common vocabulary related to the future
- Answer the question, "¿Adónde vas?"
- Answer the question, "¿Qué vas a hacer?"

Review of IR (to go)

Remember this? The verb "IR" means, "to go" in Spanish. We use IR to describe where we are going or what we are going to do. Let's learn how to conjugate this important verb in the present tense!

I go	Yo **VOY**
You go	Tú **VAS**
He / She / You (formal) goes/go	Él / Ella / Usted (Ud.) **VA**
We go	Nosotros/as **VAMOS**
You all (informal) go	Vosotros/as **VAIS**
They / You all (formal) go	Ellos / Ellas / Ustedes (Uds.) **VAN**

When we're talking about where we want to go in Spanish, we use the verb "IR" followed by the location. For example, if I want to say, "I go to the pool," it would look like this:

"Yo voy a la piscina." (I go to the pool.)

If we want to say where we are going on a certain day of the week, we use the article "el" in front of the day of the week like this:

"Yo voy a la piscina el sábado." (I go to the pool on Saturday.)

"Nosotros vamos a la piscina el viernes." (We go to the pool on Friday.)

IMPORTANT NOTE: When saying "to the," remember the following:

a + el = al… (al parque – to the park)

a + la = a la… (a la escuela – to the school)

Simple Future - "IR + a + Infinitive"

Once you know how to conjugate "IR" in the present tense, you can speak in the simple future quite easily. What is the simple future? It is a way to say what you are going to do at a later time. Simply conjugate the verb "IR" in the proper person, add "a" followed by the infinitive of any verb.

¿Qué vas a hacer?

Let's think about the following question, "¿Qué vas a hacer?" (What are you going to do?)

I am going to study. – Yo voy a estudiar.

You are going to study. – Tú vas a estudiar.

We are going to study. – Nosotros vamos a estudiar.

Or:

I am going to sing. – Yo voy a cantar.

She is going to sing. – Ella va a cantar.

They are going to sing. – Ellos van a cantar.

Verb Review

To use	Usar
To touch, to play an instrument	Tocar
To run	Correr
To read	Leer
To speak, to talk	Hablar
To write	Escribir
To swim	Nadar
To practice	Practicar
To see	Ver
To study	Estudiar

To dance	Bailar
To listen	Escuchar
To sing	Cantar
To play	Jugar
To draw	Dibujar
To eat	Comer
To ski	Esquiar
To do, to make	Hacer
To sleep	Dormir

Vocabulary of the Future

Tomorrow	Mañana
Tonight	Esta noche
This afternoon	Esta tarde
This weekend	Este fin de semana
Next week	La semana que viene
Next month	El mes que viene
Next year	El año que viene

Location Vocabulary

Library	La biblioteca
Gym	El gimnasio
Park	El parque
Beach	La playa
Cinema	El cine
Supermarket	El supermercado
School	La escuela
House	La casa
Countryside	El campo
Airport	El aeropuerto
Restaurant	El restaurante

Zoo	El zoológico / el zoo
City	La ciudad
Pool	La piscina
Party	La fiesta
Mountains	Las montañas

PRACTICE

Sit down with a friend and ask him or her the following questions:

- ¿Adónde vas este fin de semana?
- ¿Adónde vas mañana?
- ¿Adónde vas esta noche?
- ¿Adónde vas esta tarde?
- ¿Qué vas a hacer?

Lesson Summary

I can conjugate the verb **"IR"** (to go) in the present tense!

Yo **VOY** (I go), tú **VAS** (you go), él/ella/usted **VA** (he/she/you formal go), nosotros/as **VAMOS** (we go), ellos/ellas/ustedes **VAN** (they/you all go).

I can use the verb IR to speak in the simple future.

Simply conjugate the verb "IR" in the proper person, add "a" followed by the infinitive of any verb. **(IR + a + infinitive)**

I can use common Spanish vocabulary related to location.

I can use common Spanish vocabulary to talk about the future.

I can answer the question, **"¿Adónde vas?"**

I can answer the question, **"¿Qué vas a hacer?"**

¿Adónde vas esta semana?

Where are you going this week? Answer the questions based on your schedule. Follow the example.

Lunes	Martes	Miércoles	Jueves	Viernes	Sábado	Domingo
Voy a la escuela.	Voy al restaurante.	Voy a la biblioteca.	Voy al parque.	Voy al cine.	Voy a la playa.	Voy a la casa.

1. ¿Adónde vas el jueves?

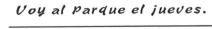 *Voy al parque el jueves.*

2. ¿Adónde vas el martes?

3. ¿Adónde vas el viernes?

4. ¿Adónde vas el lunes?

5. ¿Adónde vas el miércoles?

6. ¿Adónde vas el domingo?

7. ¿Adónde vas el sábado?

¡Voy a la playa el sábado!

¿Adónde vas?

Where are you going? Conjugate "IR" in the present tense and then fill in the blanks with the correct Spanish phrase. Follow the example.

I go	Yo	
You (familiar) go	Tú	
He / She / You (formal) go	Él / Ella / Usted	
We go	Nosotros/as	
They / You all go	Ellos / Ellas / Ustedes	

1. **You go to the cinema.**   *Tú vas al cine.*

2. **I go to the cinema.**

3. **We go to the airport.**

4. **They go to the pool**

5. **She goes to the party.**

6. **You all go to the country.**

7. **We go to the beach.**

8. **He goes to the zoo.**

9. **I go to the library.**

10. **She goes to the city.**

¡Vamos a la playa!

¿Qué vas a hacer?

What are you going to do? Answer the following questions in Spanish using a proper verb from the word bank below. Follow the example.

comer	dormir	jugar al fútbol
esquiar	nadar	ver los animales
estudiar	correr	
bailar	leer	

1. ¿Qué vas a hacer en la casa? *Voy a dormir.*

2. ¿Qué vas a hacer en la fiesta?

3. ¿Qué vas a hacer en el zoológico?

4. ¿Qué vas a hacer en la escuela?

5. ¿Qué vas a hacer en la piscina?

6. ¿Qué vas a hacer en el restaurante?

7. ¿Qué vas a hacer en las montañas?

8. ¿Qué vas a hacer en la biblioteca?

9. ¿Qué vas a hacer en el gimnasio?

10. ¿Qué vas a hacer en el parque?

¡Voy a jugar al fútbol!

UNCOVER THE HIDDEN SPANISH PHRASE

Fill in the blanks with the missing words to uncover the hidden phrase.

1. A place where I get books.

2. A place to buy groceries.

3. Where I go to see animals.

4. Where I go to watch movies.

5. Paris is the name of a...?

6. To catch a plane we go to the...?

7. How do you say, "I go" in Spanish?

8. When I want to swim I go to the...?

9. After school I go to my...?

Lesson 10 – Introduction to Spanish-Speaking Countries

What will we learn in this lesson?

By the end of this lesson, you will be able to:

- List the Spanish-speaking countries of the world
- Locate Spanish-speaking countries on a world map
- List interesting facts about Spanish-speaking countries
- Describe how widely spoken Spanish is throughout the world
- Talk to your friends and family about the language and culture of several Spanish-speaking countries

¿Sabías que? (Did you know?)

Did you know that there are 21 Spanish-speaking countries in the world? Spanish is spoken all over the world and is the second most widely spoken language in the world with over 400 million speakers! Almost all Spanish-speaking countries are located in the Americas but there is even one small Spanish-speaking country located in Africa! Let's read some fun facts about Spanish-speaking countries around the world.

Estados Unidos Mexicanos (México)

Our closest Spanish-speaking neighbor is the "United Mexican States," or more commonly referred to simply as Mexico. Did you know that Mexico is made up of 31 states and has over 100 million people? Mexico is a very popular destination for tourists from around the world and is home to many famous vacation hot spots like Cancun, Mexico City, Cabo San Lucas, and Puerto Vallarta, to name a few.

Culturally, Mexico is known for its delicious food, its iconic music, and its beautiful beaches.

FUN FACTS!

Here are some fun facts about Mexico!

1. The Chihuahua, the smallest breed of dog in the world, is named after the Mexican state, Chihuahua.

2. Mexico is the most populous Spanish-speaking country in the world.

3. Mexico City sinks 10 inches each year because was built on an ancient lake.

4. Chocolate was discovered in Mexico by the Aztecs in the 1500's.

5. Spanish conquerors introduced bullfighting to Mexico. Mexico is home to the biggest bullfighting ring in the world, the Plaza de Toros, which seats about 50,000 people.

6. The world's largest pyramid is not in Egypt, but in Mexico!

España (Spain)

The Spanish language originated in Spain, a beautiful country found in Europe rich in culture. Did you know that when you talk about "Spanish people" you're talking about people from Spain, not people who simply speak Spanish?

The capital of Spain is Madrid and is Spain's largest city, home to more than 3 million people. Spanish people are known for their love of soccer and their love of dance, specifically flamenco dance. They are also well known for their festivals. One famous festival that you may have heard of, is called the "Running of the Bulls" and takes place in Pamplona, in northern Spain.

Spanish food looks nothing like Mexican food! You'd have a hard time finding a taco or an enchilada in Spain! As a matter of fact, a "tortilla" in Spain is nothing like a Mexican tortilla. Spanish tortilla, or "tortilla española," is made of potatoes and eggs and looks more like a quiche than a Mexican tortilla. It's delicious!

FUN FACTS!

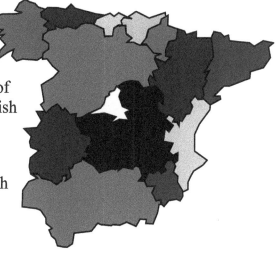

Here are some fun facts about Spain!

1. The Spanish language is spoken in many areas of the world due to the early influence of the Spanish empire.

2. The guitar was invented in Spain.

3. Spain has a royal family and a democracy, which means that the Spanish king and the Spanish president rule together.

4. Spain has a variety of unique foods and dishes such as paella (a type of rice dish) and tapas (Spanish appetizers).

5. Soccer is the most popular sport in Spain.

6. Every year, on July 6th, Spain celebrates the festival of San Fermin, or the Running of the Bulls, as it is more commonly known. A rocket is set off and men, followed by six angry bulls, run through the streets of Pamplona and eventually into a bullring.

América Central (Central America)

Central America is a tropical isthmus that connects North America to South America. It includes seven countries, all with Spanish as their primary language, with the exception of Belize where English is the primary language but where Spanish is widely spoken.

Central America, roughly the size of Texas, is made up of the following countries:

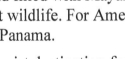

- Belize
- Guatemala
- Nicaragua
- Honduras
- El Salvador
- Costa Rica
- Panama

Central America is a land filled with Mayan ruins, beautiful tropical beaches, rainforests and abundant wildlife. For American tourists, popular destinations include Belize, Costa Rica, and Panama.

Costa Rica, a popular tourist destination for the adventurous, is particularly well known for its adventures in nature including hiking near volcanoes, zip lining, white water rafting, and exploring the rainforests.

El Caribe (The Caribbean)

The islands of the Caribbean include three Spanish-speaking countries:

- Cuba
- Puerto Rico
- Dominican Republic

Cuba

Cuba is the largest of all Caribbean islands and has a population of roughly 11 million people. Until Recently, Cuba was not accessible to American citizens due to political reasons, making travel to Cuba nearly impossible. However, recently political tensions between the United States and Cuba have improved making Cuba a potential destination for Americans and especially, Cuban Americans. Cuba is well known for its music, its old automobiles, and of course, for its cigars.

Puerto Rico

Puerto Rico is a commonwealth of the United States with a population of approximately 3.7 million people. It was originally discovered by Christopher Columbus and ruled by Spain for centuries. There are two official languages of Puerto Rico, English and Spanish. However, only a small minority of the population speaks English and Spanish is the dominant language of the island. Its capital is San Juan. Puerto Rico is well known for its beautiful beaches and its tropical climate with 70-80 degree temperatures year round. Best of all, if you live in the United States, you don't need a passport to get there!

La República Dominicana

The Dominican Republic is a Spanish-speaking nation on the island of Hispaniola. It shares this island with the nation of Haiti, which is a nation completely independent of the Dominican Republic even speaking a different language, French. The Dominican Republic is the second largest Caribbean nation after Cuba and home to nearly 10 million people. Did you know that the Dominican Republic is the most visited destination in the Caribbean? Tourists love its beaches, culture, and year-round golf courses.

América del Sur (South America)

South America is the fourth largest continent in size and the fifth largest in population. It is bordered by the Atlantic Ocean to the east and the Pacific Ocean to the west. Before South America was colonized by Europe, the ancient Incas were the dominant civilization in South America. Perhaps you've heard of Machu Picchu? Machu Picchu is a region of ancient Incan ruins located in the mountains of Peru. In the 1500's, Spain and Portugal colonized much of the area. Did you know that South America's largest country, Brazil, speaks Portuguese as its primary language?

South America is made up of the following Spanish-speaking countries:

- Venezuela

- Colombia

- Ecuador

- Peru

- Chile

- Boliva
- Paraguay
- Uruguay
- Argentina

FUN FACTS!

Here are some fun facts about South America!

1. The mighty Amazon River is located in South America.

2. The ancient Incan ruins of Machu Picchu found in Peru are considered one of the Seven Wonders of the World.

3. While South America's rainforests are some of the wettest places on Earth, the Atacama Desert in Chile is considered to be one of the driest places on Earth.

4. The largest South American country in both size and population is Brazil and its official language is Portuguese.

5. The southernmost city in the world is in South America. The city is called Ushuaia, is located in Argentina and more than 55,000 people live there.

6. Angel Falls in Venezuela are the world's highest waterfalls.

República de Guinea Ecuatorial (Equatorial Guinea)

Equatorial Guinea is a country located in Central Africa and is the only sovereign African state that speaks Spanish as its official language. It has a population of approximately 1.2 million people and is one of Africa's richest countries due to the oil it produces. However, it is considered a country with one of the worst human rights records in the world.

Lesson Summary

I can list several Spanish-speaking countries of the world!

I can locate several Spanish-speaking countries on the world map!

I can list interesting facts about many Spanish-speaking countries!

I can describe how widely spoken Spanish is throughout the world!

I can talk to my friends and family about the language and culture of several Spanish-speaking countries!

México

Color and label México.
Where would we find the
United States on this map?

How many states make up
Mexico?

España

Color and label España. For extra fun, label the country that borders Spain to the west.

On which continent do we find Spain?

América del Sur

Color and label the following SPANISH-SPEAKING countries:

ARGENTINA
PERU
BOLIVIA
CHILE
COLOMBIA
ECUADOR
PARAGUAY
URUGUAY
VENEZUELA

América Central

Color and label the following
SPANISH-SPEAKING countries:

BELIZE*
GUATEMALA
EL SALVADOR
HONDURAS
NICARAGUA
COSTA RICA
PANAMA

*The official language of BELIZE is
English but Spanish is widely
spoken.

Los Países del Mundo
Donde Se Habla Español

(The Countries of the World where Spanish is Spoken)

DIRECTIONS: Label and color the areas on this map where we would find all of the Spanish-speaking countries of the word, (A-F). A. México, B. América Central, C. El Caribe, D. América del Sur, E. España , F. República de Guinea Ecuatorial.